Love's Freedom

Summer N Dawn

Love's Freedom

Contents

To Whitney, For keeping me sane and listening to my crazy ideas!

To Shelia, I strive to be like you one day.

To the military spouses, you are never alone. Let the love and support carry you through.

TRIGGER WARNINGS

If any of the following triggers you, please refrain from reading! Your mental state matters!

TRIGGERS:
SEX
VIOLENCE
ATTEMPTED RAPE
MURDER
DEATH OF A CHILD
PUBLIC SEX
PTSD
DISACOSSIATION
ABUSE

Part One

1

Prologue- Jared

I gave ten years to the United States Army, and what do I have to show for it?

PTSD- the sleep scare kind.

Regret- missed time with my wife.

Death- Sharon would be alive today if I had come home sooner.

But now my life is different thanks to a different army.

An army that can be both good and bad.

An army that gave me a new start.

2

Jared

Sharon has been dead for four long years now.

We were high school sweethearts and married for ten years.

She loved me, even though I often chose the Army over her.

We were well off, but I was always worried about making money to support us.

The night she died, I was on my way home from a mission.

She never knew where I was until I came home from the missions.

She claimed she would worry less if she didn't know exactly where I was.

She was in a major accident and walking home from her part-time job at the bookstore.

The accident happened when a drunk driver didn't realize he had swerved onto the sidewalk.

Sharon had just walked out of the bookstore when the accident occurred.

The driver sent Sharon flying through the bookstore window.

She died on impact.

I was only gone for two months. But I returned to losing my wife.

I later found out I had lost my child, too.

Sharon was pregnant, and because of the impact, I lost Sharon and our baby girl.

If my flight hadn't been canceled the day before, I would've been home, and she would still be alive.

I will always cherish the memory of her warm embrace when I was troubled by nightmares.

I can still hear her gentle scolding about leaving my pens in my uniform and having them washed.

The aroma of her delicious chicken alfredo still lingers in my mind.

I miss the feeling of her hands washing my back in the shower and the sound of her scissors as she carefully cut my hair.

The little things mean the most, and you miss them more than you thought you could.

It started leaving flowers on their graves on the anniversary of their death.

I will sit at the cemetery and tell Sharon and my angel baby about what's happening in life.

Sitting there brings me peace, but it also doesn't let me forget what I lost.

I joined the Ballentine Bratva right after Sharon's death.

Massimo completely understood my situation.

He took me in and trusted me.

I know he looked deep into my background, and he knows everything.

He knows why I joined and left the Army and about Sharon and the baby.

I didn't think the most powerful man in Chicago would be as friendly and understanding as he is.

Ten years ago, I made the life-altering decision to enlist in the army in order to break free from the toxic environment of my home.

At the time, I was residing with my mother and father.

My father, battling alcoholism, neglected me, showing more concern for my mother.

Meanwhile, my mother, who had become accustomed to being indulged, would only attend to my needs when my father raised his voice.

Life has a crazy way of showing you what you need.

When Sharon died, I was a lost puppy.

I only did the bare minimum so that I would survive.

I was almost to the point of no return.

I felt empty, cold, and even dead.

Sharon was my life.

Even though she felt like she came second to the Army, that was never the case in my eyes.

She was the reason I got out of bed in the morning, the reason I stuck with the Army as long as I did, my heart and soul.

She made me a better person and soldier.

Not a day goes by that I wish I had a chance to save her.

An opportunity to hold her again, a chance to love her, and a chance to touch her.

Have I been looking for love since her death? No.

Has love appealed to me? Yes, love is all around me.

Massimo is married and in love with Kass.

Roman is married to Asia, who is also part of the Bratva.

Both couples give me hope.

Both women are treated like they walk on water.

They are both excellent wives and mothers; Massimo and Roman never complain about them, and they only sing their praises.

That's why I want a second chance at love.

Do I deserve to be loved again? Probably Not.

Do I fall hard or soft? With Sharon, I fell fast and hard.

We started dating, and then six months later, we were engaged.

One year after that, we were married.

Looking back, I see where Sharon felt neglected.

I didn't take the time to communicate properly with her.

I would voice my feelings and ignore hers.

She felt like her problems were Never seen or heard.

Sharon never told me this, but I found this out in her diary.

I thought reading her thoughts would comfort me, and it gave me some until I read an entry right before returning home.

It read:

Jared should be home in a few hours! I have mixed feelings about it. I'm grateful for our little girl, but I can't shake the feeling that he will prioritize the baby and his military duties over me. I miss the days when I felt like his main priority and when he showed me how much he loved me. Now, I feel like I'm just here to take care of him. I cook, clean, and put his needs before my own. I hope he'll realize how much I care for him when I'm gone. The doctors found cancer near my uterus, so there's a chance that I won't be around for long after giving birth. I hope Jared will find love again, and I hope I'll be around to see our baby grow up.

The letter was dated two days before I was set to come home.

My heart broke even more after I read that.

I pushed my wife to the point of self-doubt.

Sharon felt unwanted, and I made her feel that way.

My woman will have freedom if I get a second chance at love.

She will make all the decisions when it comes to our relationship.

I will handle the world, and she will handle the freedom of love.

Have I been lonely these last four years?

I would give anything just to have a companion.

I want someone I can talk to, someone I can hold, someone I can cherish, and someone I can look after.

That is the trend among Bratva men.

We don't have an easy life, so we make other people's lives hell or heaven.

I choose to make the ones who deserve to suffer wish they died before they met me.

Then, the ones who deserve heaven will get that.

I have secretly spoiled an Angel who does so much good.

She helps us whenever she can and helps the women's shelter whenever she has free time.

She is always taking care of others.

When was the last time she did anything for herself?

I have been sending her little by little, but I have been spoiling her for a month. I first sent my Angel a bouquet of white and red roses.

The card read:

Angel,
Take care of yourself; do more for yourself. You deserve to relax. You help care for so many people, but some would rather see you take care of yourself. So I will help you do that little by little.
Sincerely,
Freedom

Then I sent her a gift certificate to the spa with another note that Read:
Breathe in, breathe out. Your health and Sanity matters.
Love, Freedom

Now, I ensure her favorite iced coffee is delivered to work with little messages on the cup.

Like today's cup said:

Smile, love. Freedom can set you free.

Sara Rossi deserves to be spoiled and the freedom to do whatever her heart desires

3

Sara

Today is going to be busy; I feel it. I didn't have time for coffee, so let's hope my water lasts me.

As I walk into the hospital, Nurse Jane rushes to catch up.

"Doctor Sara, this coffee was delivered for you." She says.

I take it from her. It's an iced caramel coffee with extra caramel and whipped cream.

I look at Jane, "Did you order this for me, Jane?"

"I wish I could take credit, doctor. But it was delivered. There's a message on the cup."

I look at the cup, and it reads: "Smile, love. Freedom can set you free."

The words automatically make me smile.

This mysterious "Freedom" person has been sending me stuff for a while now.

"Thank you for grabbing it; I will see you on rounds."

Jane takes her leave.

I go into the physicians' lounge to relax before I clock in.

Does it scare me that "Freedom" keeps sending me gifts? No, not at all.

I am being watched constantly by the Ballentine Bratva.

They will not let anything happen to me. I am not the only doctor willing to overlook something they do, but I greatly owe them.

I owe them my life.

Massimo and one of his men saved my life. My ex-fiancé had stabbed me.

He stabbed me in the stomach, deep enough to kill my child.

I was just over one and a half months into my pregnancy.

He felt like the baby would ruin his life.

Turns out he was fucking at least three soldiers from his unit, and one of them was his commanding officer.

I swear if I see Terrence Burkes's face ever again, I will beg any of Massimo's men to end his life.

The overwhelming grief and pain that he inflicted upon me took years to overcome.

Despite the passage of time, I still make a monthly pilgrimage to our child's resting place.

I recently received word that Terrence has been deployed with the Army once again, and I sincerely hope that he never has to return to Chicago.

I implored Massimo to spare Terrence's life, but I know now that I cannot make that same mistake again.

4

Terrence

In thirty minutes, I'll be back in Chicago, marking the end of my last tour of duty.

After seven years in the Army, I've finally returned for good.

Reflecting on my time in the military, I have some regrets, such as being involved romantically with both of my commanders.

I thought I would come out of this in at least one relationship, but instead, I am back on the market.

I am too charismatic for my own good; I attract attention from both men and women.

At the moment, my focus is solely on one person.

She is unaware of my presence in the vicinity, but she will be soon.

5

Jared

I was born as Jared Carson, but in the army, everyone called me Arson.

Anytime we were under attack, or anytime it called for, I would deliberately set anything I could on fire to help out.

Now, whenever Massimo needs a cleanup crew and wants to burn things to the ground, he calls Arson.

No matter what, I will not fail him.

After Sharon's death, I almost succeeded in killing myself.

I was outside an abandoned building that was about to be demolished in two days. I had my trusty lighter in my hand. The plan was to go inside, set the place on fire, and never come back out.

After reading her diary, I felt like I had ruined a wonderful woman. I never got the chance to make it up, to comfort her, or to show her what she really meant to me.

If she couldn't walk this earth, I shouldn't either.

Just as I had walked into the building, a shadow followed me. That shadow was Massimo.

I remember the conversation like it was yesterday.

"Whatever you are thinking, stop, don't do it. I know you're trying to kill yourself. It's not worth it. I've done my research, and I know what you've been through. Help me work for me. We will find your purpose. We will work together to make you feel like you belong. You always have a choice, and I'll never make you do anything you don't want to." Massimo's voice had a calming effect on me.

I retorted, "Why should I? How will you make me feel like I belong in this world? I have lost everything. I don't belong in this world. My wife is dead, and if my plane had been on time, I could've saved her. She was my world. She was my freedom. But that has been snatched away from me."

Massimo touches my shoulder, "You will be by my side. I am the leader of the Ballentine Bratva, and we run Chicago. But we also make those who need to pay. We do both legal and non-legal work. You tell me where you want to fall, and that's where you'll stay. If you want to stay on the side, you can be legal, or if you want to deal with drugs and other black market stuff, you can. Don't let your training go to waste. Let me help you, join my family. If you do, you'll never suffer again and have a band of brothers behind you again. What do you say, Arson?"

He knew everything about me, and he taught me everything. He saved me.

I pose as his driver, but I'm his protection and intelligence. I'm always alert and on guard.

I never go inside his building unless it's an emergency or my two days off.

On my days off, he has another protector, his wife.

Kassani doesn't let him leave the house if I'm off unless Roman can accompany him.

I want a woman who cares for me like that and wants to ensure I'm always safe.

Tonight, I'm headed out with my band of brothers.

It's time to celebrate.

There has been no crime or sex tracking in the last six months.

Finally, we can breathe a little, but not too much.

I will limit myself to one drink.

I will always protect my brothers.

They deserve this freedom.

6

Terrence

I watched as Sara walked out of the hospital, her white coat billowing behind her in the breeze.

It baffled me why she persisted in pursuing her medical career when she clearly belonged at home, tending to my needs.

I couldn't help but notice that she had put on at least twenty pounds since we were last together.

Four years of being apart was far too long.

I was determined to bring her back into my embrace.

She was the best woman I ever had, but she needs to understand that even though I am with her, I will do whatever I want.

When we were together in the past, she couldn't understand that I was allowed to be with anyone I wanted, even if I was in a relationship.

Women have no say in what men do.

Women belong at our feet, fulfilling our wants and desires without giving us any attitude.

Women are weak.

This woman will do as I say.

7

Sara

Today's shift was a doozy.

Two people tried to die in my care today, but I didn't let that happen.

Anytime I can save a patient I will, I never want to be the reason a life ends.

I had Massimo send someone to pick up my car, I just need to walk home.

I need to clear my mind.

Today took a toll on me; I have not handled death well ever since I lost my baby.

Does Terrence feel remorse?

Does he miss our baby?

Does he have kids now?

Did he change his ways?

Would I take him back? No chance in hell will he ever win me over again.

If I do see him, he better not piss me off, or I will get Massimo involved.

I don't think Terrence understands the damage he did.

I will never be able to have children again. To save my life, they had to remove my uterus and remove my tubes.

My dreams of motherhood may never come true, but I have come to terms with that.

There are so many beautiful babies in this world already, and I get to be involved with two of them.

Warren Hart Ballentine and Kassie Hart, their mothers, had a challenging and complicated birth. But both children and mothers are doing fantastic. I go over and see them at least once a month.

Babies are only little for so long we must cherish it.

I know I watched by Massimo's men, but tonight it feels like there are an extra set of eyes on me.

Maybe it's nothing, I just need to get home.

8

Terrence

She's on edge as she walks home.

She keeps looking back like someone is following her.

She is right.

I just need to know where she lives.

I have a new job and will ensure I can work in her neighborhood.

She may not know it yet, but she is still MINE.

Nothing will stand in my way.

I spent seven years in the Army as MOS 11B.

I know how to shoot and kill.

I will not hesitate to kill for my women, touch them, and die.

Touch them, and I will bury you myself.

9

Jared

Why is Massimo texting me this late?

Something must be going on.

The text reads:
"Get Sara's car, it's at the hospital. She had a bad night; make sure she is okay."

Angel had a lousy night?

I reply, "OMW, Boss."

I am going to bring her donuts, two dozen worth.

Massimo said he had seen her eat a whole box when she had a bad day.

She deserves to smile.

I will try my hardest to get a glimpse of that angelic smile.

10

Sara

Being a doctor was my dream, but after today, I'm spent.

I hate losing people; even though today they pulled through, it takes a toll on me.

I no longer feel the extra eyes piercing my skin as I enter my apartment.

Who would care enough, besides Massimo's men, to try to get that close to me?

None comes to mind.

Terrence doesn't care.

He disappeared right after I got out of the hospital.

It's been radio silence from him.

The graves keeper said another and I were the only people visiting baby Rossi's grave.

I showed them a picture of Terrence, and they said that wasn't him, so who could be visiting my baby's grave?

I couldn't bring myself to name her, so I just gave her my last name.

I visit her twice a month.

I head into my lonely room, where my generic bed and nightstand sit.

I just sleep in here, so I keep it organized and bare.

But I do keep two knives in my nightstand.

 I can't sleep if they are not there.

If anything tries to occur, I am prepared.

I may be a doctor, but there are people out there who have no respect for the lives of others, and I just want to protect myself.

I am not ready to die; there is too much to do in this world to make it better. I will do my part until the day I perish.

11

Jared

I finally made it to Angel's apartment.

I am armed with my knife and gun like always, but today, I'm also armed with flowers and two dozen donuts.

She deserves the world, and I never want to see her frown.

I knock on her door. I hear her feet running across the room to answer the door.

I hide my face with the flowers.

She swings the door open. "I didn't order anything. If you tell me what address you are looking for, I will help you find it."

She looks like she rushed to dry off just to answer the door.

Her hair is wrapped in a silky blue towel that matches her blue pajamas.

I remove the flowers from my face and give her my hidden southern accent, "Sorry to bother Ms. Sara. Massimo told me to drop your car off, so I came to bring you your keys. He always said you had a rough day, ma'am. So I stopped off and got you some flowers and your favorite donuts. Sorry if I overstepped."

She blinks rapidly like there's something in her eye, "Jared, that's so sweet of you! You got my favorite flowers and donuts. Thank you so much! Yes, I did have a bad day, but it looks like you turned it around. Would you like to come in? Only if you are not on duty, I don't want to interfere with your work."

I can hear what she is saying, but I'm distracted by the fact that her nipples are standing at attention.

Well, I'll be damn, she might be attracted to me.

I clear my throat, "I would love to, ma'am, but only if I'm not messing up your routine."

Sara smiled and shivered, "Not at all, honey! Come inside and enjoy these donuts with me."

As I entered Sara's apartment, I noticed how clean and organized it was.

Not a thing was out of place. There were no dishes in the sink, and there was not even a speck of dust in the living room.

Massimo told me Sara refused the apartment he offered at his complex.

She told him she needed her privacy, especially since she would be coming and going all night.

Of course, he set her up with this apartment, but does she know it's in her name?

It's considered an apartment, but she's the owner.

Massimo wanted to make sure that she was taken care of, so she owns her apartment and six others on the street where she lives.

Massimo says she never checks her bank account, so she hasn't become suspicious yet, but he had the lawyers take care of everything. If she wanted to, she'd never have to be a doctor again. She could sit back, relax, and put her feet up.

The rent for one apartment alone is $4500 a month. She makes $22,500 a month without doing anything.

She doesn't even realize she doesn't have to pay rent because it's her apartment complex.

Not only did Massimo set this up because Sarah is our on-call doctor, but she's also one of our rescues.

He told me everything that happened with her ex, and her ex had better not show his face around here.

Sara doesn't realize how similar we are; we have both lost children.

But most of all, we want to be valued and loved again.

Massimo said Sarah's been talking with Kassani and Asia about possibly finding love again.

I hope Sarah finds a man who treats her like she should be treated, like an angel.

If she was my angel, she would never want for anything, and no tears would ever be shed.

"I love your place. Did you decorate it yourself?" I ask.

She giggles, "No, your boss had a designer come in and do it all to my specifications. It was lovely of him. But the whole blue theme and flag art was my idea."

There is American flag art all over her apartment.

There are two big flag paintings, one in the living room and one in the kitchen.

At least six metal art pieces are throughout the apartment, including the one hanging over her fireplace.

"The art is beautiful. Why all the flags?"

She sighed, "I have always loved our beloved country, but I was also a Navy brat. My mom served in the Navy for fifteen years until she was killed in the line of duty. She was a Navy doctor on the way to operate on a seaman when they were attacked overhead. She was shot straight through the head, dead on impact. I had just turned eighteen when it happened. I forced my father to let me see her before they sealed the casket. Her wound lives rent-free in my head; she's why I became a doctor. I just wish I would've enlisted. Sorry, I got a little bit off track. But flags are now my favorite thing; I even have a tattoo. All flags bring me back to my hero, my mom."

Tattoo?

Where is it?

She plops down on a kitchen bar stool, sniffs and eats her donuts.

She picks up the Bavarian cream donut, and as it touches her tongue, a moan slips from her lips.

Can she moan like that for me and not the donut?

I slyly adjust my crotch, "You really like those donuts, don't you, sweetheart?"

The euphoric look stays on her face as she retorts, "Donuts are better than sex toys. Donuts never disappoint or run out of batteries. Donuts are the only reliable pleasure device."

Did she mean to let that slip?

What sounds could I make slip from those lips?

12

Sara

Did I really just say that?!

I have only written that in my journal and never said it out loud!

Oh my goodness, he's going to think I am a total dingbat!

Did he just adjust his pants?

Oh my goodness!

Could he be attracted to me?

I squeal, "I am so sorry, but ignore that comment! I am so embarrassed! It just slipped out before I could stop it! I promise I am an intelligent woman!"

I cover my face with my hands.

He probably thinks I have lost my mind.

As I sit up to look at him, my pajama strap falls off my shoulder.

Oh shit!

Jared is looking at me like he wants to eat me!

I just might let him now; it's been over four years since I felt a man's touch.

13

Terrence

Is she fucking serious right now?

Who the fuck did she just let into her house?

That better be a relative.

I didn't know she had changed so much.

Could Sara be in a relationship?

NO!

She wouldn't betray our love!

How does this man know what she likes?

If he's not a relative, there's no way he would be with a working woman.

Working women are a crime!

Women belong in the kitchen.

I will stay right here and wait for him to leave.

I can end him with one shot if it comes down to it.

I now have two targets in my sights.

14

Jared

This woman and her mouth are delightful!

She has nothing to be embarrassed about; I would like to test her theory.

"Now, little lady, don't be shy! Do you want to test your theory? I bet I can bring you more pleasure than a B.O.B. What do you say, sweetheart? No strings attached unless you want them."

Let's see where she takes this; I won't pressure her.

I hope I am correctly interpreting the tension in the room.

She stares at me; I can't tell if she's excited or repulsed.

She fixes her fallen strap and replies, "Jared, are you asking little ole me to share a bed with you, sir?"

That cute little forced southern drawl gets me.

I growl, "That's precisely what I am asking, darling. Call me sir again, and I will show you where you belong."

Excitement clicks in her eyes, "Do your worst, sir!"

15

Sara

Is this 6-foot muscular man attracted to this 200-pound nerdy doctor?

Please tell me I'm not reading the signs wrong.

He's flirting with me and even teasing me.

I have not felt a man's touch in over four years.

Do I even remember what to do?

Jared has always been a sweet soul.

I remember the first day we met.

It was one month after the incident with my ex.

I looked like trash, and I felt like I had been hit by a train. But according to Jared, that's not what he saw.

I remember what he said word for word: "You are not broken. You are beautiful. You are not a disaster; you are a work in progress. Your eyes may not sparkle now, but they will sparkle soon. Your circumstances don't define you. What you make of them does."

His words and all of Massimo's help enabled me to finish the last two months of my residency and become a full-fledged doctor.

Jared's first impression sticks with me. All my life, I wanted to feel like I mattered and that I was not an object.

With those simple words, I felt like I mattered.

I wonder what this countryman can do to me with his body since even his words excite me!

Please, lord, let him ravage me!!

He hasn't moved yet.

I repeat myself, "Do your worst, sir! I'll be at your mercy."

Before I even finish my sentence, he comes around the bar and ravages me with his kisses.

His moist and tender lips are drifting me into another world!

It's almost as if I am free from the past.

16

Jared

Sara wants me!

I'm going to give her the ride of her life!

Her lips belong with mine.

Never have I tasted lips as intoxicating as hers.

Her body fits perfectly in mine. She responds to my kiss so enthusiastically that it makes me feel like I am the only one in her sights.

I caress her cheek as we kiss, trying to be dominant but gentle.

I growl at her, "Sweetheart, do you want tender loving or rough, no turning back loving? I am all about equal pleasure."

She wiggles her sexylicious body against mine, "Fire me up, Jared. I am at your mercy. I may not have much sexual experience, but I know how to take direction. Direct me, boss me, please?!"

Her little wiggle and her strong words have my cock bursting at the seams.

"Your wish will be granted, sweetheart."

I slide my hand down the inside of her pajama shorts and grip her ass for dear life.

I growl, "From this moment on, you don't speak, sweetheart. Nod if you understand." She quickly nods. "If at any point you want me to stop, just bite me, and if you want to come, just tap my back three times. This takes the guesswork out of sex, and you can focus on your pleasure. Are you ready to be proven wrong? Are you ready to find out how much pleasure I can give you?"

Sarah nods.

"Lead me to your bedroom, sweetheart. A woman like you deserves our first time to be in a proper bed."

She leads me to her bedroom. The first thing I notice is the bareness of the room. The living room makes you feel welcomed and at peace.

The bedroom is gray and emotionless, I wonder why.

Massimo said the only time she shows emotion is when she is with his and Roman's babies.

Is her bedroom void of emotion because of her ex?

Let's not overthink this.

Lets pleasure the angel, and make her feel like she's in heaven.

17

Terrence

What the fuck am I hearing?

Sara is moaning her head off.

I am sure the neighbors can hear her, too.

But I am right up against her bedroom window.

She is not saying anything.

Sounds like old dude is barking orders at her.

She never sounded like that with me, and she constantly moaned lightly or not at all.

There is no way this old man is better in bed than me!

We would always be done with our love-making in fifteen minutes.

Sara and old man have been going at it for over thirty minutes!

He says, "You like that, angel? Nod if you want it faster. I will give you everything you want! Fuck! You are so wet. Can you handle me, baby? Are you ready to come? No? Fuck, baby! I love your energy."

What in the fuck?

It's like she is letting him do whatever he wants to her!

What kind of slut has she become?

Where is my sweet missionary, Sarah?

She never liked when we changed anything in the bedroom.

Why is she being like this with this old man?

He has to be at least five years older than her.

Why does he keep talking?

"That's it, baby! Take all of me! I am flipping you over; I want you from behind! When you are close, tap my hand."

Why are they so fast and loud?

Do women actually like to be bossed in the bedroom?

Gross, their moans are making me want to kill both of them.

Maybe I will fuck her and make him watch.

The old man doesn't know what I am capable of.

"Okay, angel. I feel you. Let's come together. I want to hear you, don't hold back! Let the pleasure set you free."

This is so disgusting.

At least it is over after forty-five minutes of sex.

It won't take me that long to get pleasure from watching them suffer.

Sara will be mine again, or she will die.

18

Sara

What kind of sex was that?

I was completely relaxed.

My mind wasn't even focused on anything other than the sex, that's never happened to me before.

The pleasure was intense.

Never had I ever been able to orgrasm four times in one session.

Jared knows how to please a woman.

I couldn't control my body or my emotions, everything was intensified.

With Terrence, I never felt the connection and I always had to bring myself to completion.

I feel like Terrence was only there for his pleasure and not mine.

Jared kisses my forehead, "Angel, do you want me to stay or go?"

Seriously?

He's asking me and not just doing whatever he wants?

That is definitely new to me.

I purr, "Darling, you can stay. I'm off work. No need to rush away unless you're on the clock."

He smiles, "I'm yours until you throw me out, Angel."

"Okay, Jared, you can stay until I go back to work. But don't get too comfortable. I am not ready to put a label on us."

19

Jared

I spent the last two days with Sara, she had to go back to work today so I gave her the space she needed.

I found her tattoo.

Her upper back is adorned with a vivid and detailed depiction of a cracked American flag, situated just below her shoulder blade.

When I flipped her over, seeing the tattoo turned me on even more.

Sara is a gorgeous and intelligent woman.

She knows exactly what she wants.

We are keeping things unlabeled, as she would say.

I will wait, even if Sara is not the one I might be ready to get back out there.

But I will give this time; I want to see where Sarah wants to take this.

I pulled out my phone and ordered Sarah's coffee for delivery.

The note reads:
It's time to give myself away. I enjoyed our time together. Next time, I will bring more donuts.
Love, Freedom

The ball is in her court, game on love.

Part Two

20

Terrence

For two days, the elderly gentleman chose not to depart.

After hearing what I heard, I don't think he can be called a gentleman; bastard is more fitting.

I never thought I would see the day Sara decided that a man other than me was welcome in her home.

This will not last long. I know how to end this.

I still have ties with a bookie, and I know Sarah's dad still gambles.

I quickly text Mark, and he responds right away.

I'm on my way to meet him now.

Sara's dad will visit her very soon if everything goes as planned.

21

Sara

As I arrived at the hospital, Jane handed me my coffee and went to do her rounds.

Who is Freedom?

Why does he keep spoiling me?

The note today reads:
Time to give myself away. I enjoyed our time together. Next time I will bring more donuts.
Love, Freedom

What?

Freedom is Jared?!

No way!

That is so sweet though, and at least I am not being stalked.

This day just got better.

Before stashing my phone away, I make sure to send a quick text to Massimo, asking for Jared's phone number.

I'm feeling grateful and eager to express my appreciation to him and organize our next meet-up.

I'm feeling energized and prepared to tackle anything that comes my way today.

22

Jared

I'm on my way to my monthly therapy appointment.

It's been a routine since I was diagnosed with PTSD and dissociative disorder.

Ever since Sharon passed away, I've noticed my emotional detachment.

I remember standing at her funeral, looking at her casket without shedding a single tear.

It's been four years of therapy now, and my therapist mentioned that my disassociation is linked to my PTSD.

I've felt detached from my emotions for so long.

Lately, though, I've started to feel some progress in therapy.

Lately, I've been experiencing a significant shift in my emotional state.

I find myself becoming more open, and emotions that I kept buried deep inside are starting to surface.

Reflecting on Sharon's tragic passing has made me realize the mistakes I made in our relationship.

If I could go back, I would make things right.

However, I hope to use the lessons I've learned to improve any future relationships.

Sara is truly special; there's no one else like her.

Sara's selfless nature reminds me of Sharon.

Both of them always prioritize others' needs above their own.

That's why I won't let Sara do that, even if I have to tie her down to make her relax.

I have an appointment to attend.

I see a therapist once a month as per Massimo's request, ever since I was diagnosed with PTSD and dissociative disorder.

After Sharon passed away, I realized that I never displayed any emotions.

I didn't shed a tear at her funeral.

I just stood there, gazing at her casket.

I have been attending therapy for four years now.

The therapist mentioned that my dissociation is linked to my PTSD.

I have been detached from my emotions for years.

Lately, I've found therapy to be really helpful.

I've been able to open up more, and I'm starting to confront and process the emotions I've been keeping inside.

I've had eight therapy sessions so far, and I only have four more to go before I don't have to have weekly check-ins with my therapist anymore.

If I could turn back time, I would know how to mend it.

I hope to apply what I've learned to any future relationships.

If I can learn what steps I need to take to heal, Angel can, too.

23

Terrence

Four weeks later....

I always follow through with my plans.

I visited Sarah's dad.

I took the long journey to Mississippi.

He was not happy to see me.

I let him know that he better hurry before they come to collect his debt.

Mark informed me that her dad's debt totals over $250,000.

Sara is now on her way to Mississippi because her dear old dad did not want to tell her what was happening over the phone.

Mark will take care of him if he doesn't come up with the money in two to five days.

Sara, I know is not going to be able to pay the debt.

So she may just have to get married to save dear old dad.

Come running back into my arms, Sara.

I'll be waiting.

Then you'll be the obedient little woman you are supposed to be.

24

Sara

My dad rarely reaches out to ask me to return home.

It must be something significant because I haven't visited Mississippi in nearly eight years.

When my baby passed away, my dad came down to be by my side for six months.

He tends to prefer his solitary life away from the hustle and bustle of the city.

Dad called me a few days ago, saying he had something urgent to discuss.

So here I am, hopping on a plane to Gulfport, Mississippi.

This past month has been hectic.

Jared has been living with me, which I like.

We made it official about two weeks ago, so Jared is my boyfriend.

But he has become my protector, too.

Random gifts still appear at my house, but not from Jared or Freedom.

All the cards are signed "From TOP," I didn't know what TOP meant until Jared explained it to.

Top is what they refer to the first sergeant in the military.

I have never met a first sergeant, so I don't know who could be doing these things.

It's not things that could hurt me that they're leaving, but it is things that only someone who knows me intimately would leave.

The first thing they left was a replica of the Navy ship that my mom died on; Jared had to hold me all night long because I couldn't stop crying.

The next item that showed up was a baby rattle, taking everything too far.

You can mess with me, but you will not mess with my child.

The final item that showed up was a torn flag, which made no sense.

Unless they were just trying to make fun of my love of patriotism.

Due to these circumstances, Massimo decided that I should not travel alone.

Beside me on this flight is a large, imposing man who seems ready to take on the world on my behalf.

I can't stop picturing his body, I wake up to it every morning.

But my new favorite thing is taking a shower with him.

His chest, chiseled like a work of art, is complemented by muscular arms.

The brown and red beard that frames his face is just what the doctor ordered.

It's like Jared is my freedom and the man of my dreams.

He treats me like a treasure, like the nickname he calls me, Angel.

I don't know much about his upbringing so I'm scared for him to see my hometown.

I didn't have the best life growing up, especially after I lost my mom.

But I'm not too worried because Jared has told me he didn't have the best upbringing either.

I'm still super nervous, though.

The last time I brought a man to meet my dad, that didn't go over well.

When Terrence met dad, dad sent Terrence running, Dad doesn't beat around the bush.

Terrence didn't like the fact that my dad told him he could not support me and that I wasn't a woman to be tamed.

Terrence argued that love can change any woman.

My dad told him that may be the case for most women, but it was not going to work for me.

The bond between my father and me has always been strong.

The only event that caused a rift in our closeness was my mom's passing.

Dad didn't know how to cope; he just wanted to be alone and reminisce about the times they had.

When he refused my offer to let him move in with me, I told him I would take care of him for the rest of his life, and he would never have to worry again.

Dad has become a recluse; the only time he comes to see me is at Christmas.

And that's because I refuse to let him sit at home alone on what used to be his favorite holiday.

Stepping off the plane, I already smell the saltwater in the air; it's not clean saltwater.

It smells like a dusty house and a little feet mixed with salt and onions.

It makes me cherish the city that I'm in now.

As we got into the Uber, Jared turned to me, "Angel, I didn't know this is where you were from. I was stationed here for three years at Keesler Air Force Base. We could've met sooner."

Um, why is my heart beating out of my chest?

Why do I feel like I am the only thing he sees?

"Jared, that is sweet. But if we had met, I promise we would not be where we are today. From what you said then, you were still married, and I didn't know what I wanted from this life. I was still struggling with the abuse and losing my baby girl. But now I feel free like my freedom is because of you. I am excited for you to meet my dad. He can be a real hard ass. But if he likes you, then he is a cuddly teddy bear. He's going to love you."

25

Terrence

She took that bastard with her!

Why the hell would she bring him to meet Eric?

It doesn't matter; Eric Rossi is going to run him off.

Or at least he better.

Eric Rossi is not as tough as he used to be; I could take him down.

I explained the situation to him; all he had to do was get her married so her husband could pay off his debts.

I pointed my gun to his head and made sure he knew that I was the only candidate to marry Sara or I would come back for him.

This is the best way to get my Sara back.

She will be the way I want, not the way this old man has made her.

I need her to be obedient and docile.

My women don't fight...they surrender.

26

Sara

Pulling up to Dad's apartment complex, we immediately notice it looks run down.

The grass outside is overgrown, vines cover the entire complex, and cracks run down the side of the building.

As we walk in, we smell the moldy air filled with dust.

How is Dad living here?

How does he breathe in here?

Jared whispered, "We need to get your dad out of here. If he isn't already sick, he will be. I'm texting Massimo now to see if we have an apartment open."

I sigh, "Darling, I don't know if Dad will leave with us. Let's see what he says, and we can go from there."

Jared slips his arms around me, "Yes, dear, you know best."

I am not used to this relationship dynamic.

With Terrence, he would boss and control me in the bedroom and out.

Terrence ensured I met his demands and never cared about what I wanted or needed.

In the short time Jared and I have been together, he has only focused on me, as if he doesn't care about his needs.

He always ensures my comfort and never forces me to do anything I don't want to.

We take turns making dinner, and he helps with all the housework.

It seems he's my Mr. Right; no, my Mr. Freedom.

When Massimo asked Jared if he had told me his history, Jared responded, "Sara brings out the honesty in me. She is the first person I have felt safe with in a long time."

I felt myself swoon.

I never felt like I was that important to anyone except my dad.

Freedom is sweet.

27

Jared

Sara has nothing to be ashamed of; my upbringing was worse than hers.

She had the love of both parents, and I had neither.

Massimo had me do a thorough background check on her dad, his debts belong to us.

I need to tell Sara before she gets the wrong idea.

"Angel, before we go in there, I wanted to let you know that Massimo and I ran a background check, and we know what your dad wants to talk about."

She looks at me with worry, "What is it? How bad is it?"

I slip my arm around her shoulders. "He's in debt about $250,000. He acquired all that debt when he stayed with you after you lost the baby. He gambled it away and took out a loan with one of our bookies. Apparently, someone who didn't have the authority to collect on his debt has visited your dad. We will take care of his debt, but we must figure out who is threatening you and your family."

All the tension in her body was finally released. "Okay, this is something we can work with. I will be able to pay it back soon. I should have at least half of it in savings. Thank goodness for you and Massimo finding out what is going on."

I smirk, "Angel, you should probably check your bank account. If you wanted to stop working, you could. Also, has your landlord come to visit lately?"

She sighs, "I forget you and Massimo know everything. Firstly, I am pretty sure I don't have that much money in the bank. Second, no I haven't seen the landlord in years. Why do you ask?"

I chuckle, "Angel, Massimo made you the landlord years ago. We have men come by and fix things anytime there's an issue. You haven't noticed, but rent stopped getting drafted out years ago, and everyone's payments have been coming in at the first of the month. We both care about you and want to ensure you are cared for. I am sorry. I know this is a lot of stuff to drop on you, but I want you to know everything. The Bratva will not let anything happen to you, nor will I let anything happen to you. Massimo has already sent men ahead of us to protect your dad, and he gave the go-ahead to move your father where you want."

She exclaimed, "You Bratva men don't do anything half-assed, do you? I will tell Massimo thank you, but geez, I don't need passive income."

I chuckle, "We know Angel. That's why we waited to tell you. I shouldn't tell you that Massimo has been slipping extra money in your account anytime you come to help us or the women."

"Okay, you can shut up now! Let's go see my dad, I'll sort everything out with Massimo later."

"Yes my Angel." I retorted.

I watch her ass sway from side to side, and the pride I feel watching her walk is endless.

So this is love, so this is freedom.

28

Terrence

I'm watching the old man and Sara like a hawk.

I'm hidden in the apartment's security room.

If only the sound on these stupid cameras worked.

They were talking in the hallway so intimately.

I want to kill the old man.

Sara needs someone her age, not a sugar daddy.

That has to be the only reason she's with him.

It's not the sex; that sex sounded lame and immoral.

Just wait, my dear Sara, and I will set you free.

29

Sara

Dad's apartment is a disaster.

Beer bottles are all over the floor, and dirty dishes cloud the sink.

There is a musty smell throughout the whole apartment.

Dad has not been taking care of himself, as you can clearly see.

Mom's death did a complex number on him.

"Dad, where are you? What did you need to talk about?" I exclaimed.

Dad comes running for the bedroom, "Oh, my baby! Thank goodness you're safe!

Dad smothers me with hugs and kisses.

I can smell the pungent smell of whiskey and beer mingling together.

Dad notices Jared, "Who's your friend, honey? With that full designer suit on, he sticks out like a sore thumb."

I can tell by the way dad is looking at Jared. He may not like Jared.

He's looking at Jared like he's a piece of meat ready to slaughter.

But I also see the sadness in Dad's eyes; I can't stand to see my dad sad.

"Dad, this is Jared, my boyfriend. Jared, this is my dad, Eric Rossi."

Dad exclaimed, "Boyfriend? No way end it now!"

Dad looks distraught, "Why dad? What happened?"

Dad sighed, "Sweetheart, I am in debt. I gambled away $250,000 when I stayed with you. One of the bookies came here and visited me. I didn't know he was a bookie because the only other time I had seen him was when I was with you. I thought nothing of it when I let him into my home."

Are you kidding?

Dad knew the person who came here as a bookie?

That's odd because I don't hang out with people.

"Who was it, dad? How did they know you?"

He glances at the floor, "It was your ex-fiance, Terrence. He came here, put a gun to my head, and said if I didn't pay within 2-5 days, they would come here and kill me unless you could pay the debt. But he gave another option too, but I told him to go to hell since he wasn't there for you after the baby's death."

Terrence has lost his mind!

He will die.

I will not let Massimo spare him again.

Nobody threatens my family.

I can't believe he dares to show his face around my father.

My hand's bunch by my side, I feel myself getting ready to lash out.

Then a pair of solid and comforting arms wrap around my waist.

A charming, southern accent replies, " Mr. Rossi, you worry, we will take care of everything. We have the resources to help you and your daughter. But what did Terrence say to you? What was the other option he gave you? Was he threatening Sara?"

Dad looks like the world's weight has been lifted off his shoulders. "If my daughter trusts you, I trust you. I can see she's different with you than she ever was with that no-good man. He said he would take Sara as payment if we couldn't pay the money. But she would have to marry him as soon as possible."

Yep, that's it.

Terrence is gone certifiably insane.

Terrence better hope Massimo or Jared gets to him before I do.

I would rather be 6 feet under, lying next to my baby, than marry that monster.

30

Jared

Angel stills in my arms.

Then I feel her power surge.

"Daddy, he's not ever getting me back! We will pay your debts, and you'll move in with me! I have an extra room. We will get you out of the hell hole, but there are rules in my house. You can drink sparingly, and you must help around the house. Deal?"

Eric slouches, "Yes, sweetheart. I won't let you down."

That's my bossy girl.

I massaged her shoulders. "I called the cleaning crew. If you can pack up what you want to bring, Mr. Rossi, Sara and I will be back in the morning to leave."

Eric nods and holds out his hand for me to shake.

We make peace; he winks at me blessing Sara and I.

As we exit Eric's apartment, Angel says, "Is it safe to leave him?"

I caress her back, "Yes, Angel. It's not a regular cleaning crew coming. I already have men stationed in the lobby and inside and outside the complex."

She sighs, "Okay, Freedom. Where are we headed?"

She has only taken to calling me that recently, it's like she sees me as her freedom.

To me, Angel or love has a nice ring to it.

I don't want to scare her, but I do love her.

If she lets me, I'll keep her and cherish her forever.

"Are you up for an adventure, love?"

She looks at me with wild curiosity, "What do you have in mind, sir?"

My cock stiffens, "Exactly what you are thinking, love. Massimo just opened a club about 30 minutes from here in Biloxi. Tonight is watch and play night."

Her curiosity spikes, "You mean a sex club? How would Massimo open one down here?"

I nod, "Yes, Angel. That's why he's been traveling a lot this past month. It's called Kastaways. It's a normal club up top, but you have to be a VIP member to get into the bottom floor. There's a stage where a couple plays and there are cubicles that you can watch from, they are have a button so if you don't want people to watch you, we flip the switch and you're in a private space watching the couple and playing with your partner. It's a very safe environment, which was Kass's idea. You want to play, Angel?"

Her breath hitches, "Let's go, sir! I can handle you and all your kinks. People can watch, but I don't share! You're mine, no one else's."

Damn my woman is territorial.

It's hot as shit.

"Let's go, Angel. I'm about to take you on the ride of your life."

She jumps into my arms, "Give me a ride, Freedom. Let's see if you can handle me once you set my kinks free."

I crush my lips to hers; tonight is going to be an unforgettable night.

Love and Freedom are out on the town.

31

Terrence

They are heading to Kastaways!

How the fuck does an old man like know about the underground sex club?

What is he turning my sweet Sara into?

I'll call my playmate.

We will put our disguises on and head there.

I'm not letting them out of my sight.

He better not ruin my perfect Sara.

I like watching other couples play, but I can't understand why Sara wants to play.

Well, at least I'll get a decent fuck out of watching them.

I stole a VIP card, so this should be a fun stakeout.

Thirty minutes later...

Me and my plaything arrive at Kastaways.

My inside man who is already here said Sara, and the old man just arrived and are in the middle cubicle closest to the stage.

They just got their drinks and chocolate-covered bananas, my source says.

If Sara can't have donuts she always gets chocolate-covered bananas, she says they calm her nerves.

We get the cubicle right next to them.

Let's hope I get to watch, but my shy Sara might get cold feet.

32

Sara

This club is very classy upstairs, and the underground has a dungeon feel.

Am I nervous?

No, I have always wanted to explore my fetishes.

Freedom has slowly introduced me to different things.

I like it when he takes control.

I like it when he gets rough.

I love it when he spanks me!

I love riding him until he throws me off and climbs on top of me so he cums instantly.

I love how wet he makes me.

I like ass play, I don't know what it is, but it makes me so wet, feeling his girth and balls ramming my ass.

I can't get enough of him kissing all over my body.

Jared is not afraid to take what he wants, but he always makes sure I get full pleasure, too.

Sex has never been this fun and entertaining for me.

I'm coming out of my boring shell.

The lights dim; there are small lights in our cubicle.

The couple on stage wastes no time.

The man rips open his partner's shirt and devours her neck.

He pulls the zipper down on the front of her skirt.

I look at Freedom.

He's sitting on the blue leather couch, just watching my reaction.

I looked away too long.

The couple has already taken it to the next level, they are both naked.

The man lubricates a sizeable blue vibrator and brings the woman to the brink of ecstasy.

I look back at Freedom, and I can tell he's aroused.

He grumbles, "Do you people to watch us, love? Or do you want privacy?"

I don't answer him.

I tie my hair up in a ponytail and unzip my pink cocktail dress.

I stand before him, free and naked.

I see the couple behind Freedom watching my every move.

This is exhilarating!

I crawl to Jared, and I unzip his pants.

His cock is bulging and glistening with precum.

I don't hesitate; he loves my lips around his girth.

I have no gag reflex, he fucking loves it.

I love getting him right to the edge and then stopping, only to ride him until he bursts.

That's my plan right now.

He is moaning like there's nowhere else he could be right now.

He locks his hands in my hair; he starts to roughly guide me by pulling my hair.

That's the first sign he's getting close.

Not even six minutes later, he starts mumbling, "Fuck! Fuck yeah. Ooh, just like that love."

That's the second sign, I immediately stop and jump on his cock.

"Fuck, love! You want me to paint your insides white?" He moans.

"Come for me, Freedom. I'm going to milk your dick dry!"

As his orgasm builds, he slips one hand around my neck.

Fuck, he knows what I like!

I feel my pussy clamping down on his dick, I'm so fucking close.

He uses his index finger from his other hand and inserts it into my ass.

Fuck!

This man drives me crazy!

I completely forgot about the couple on stage, I glance over.

The woman is watching us as her partner eats her out.

She's using our scene to get off faster.

Being watched makes my juices flow.

I feel my orgasm building, I know Freedom is close.

I grip his sexy beard and ruggedly kiss him.

We climax together.

Fuck!

I just squirted!

I'm so embarrassed!

I bury my face in his neck, "Fuck, I'm so sorry! I didn't mean to squirt!"

Freedom chuckles, "Love, don't apologize! That was the sexiest thing I have ever seen. I love you, Angel."

He likes that I squirted all my juice onto him!

Damn, that's hot!

I don't have to hide.

He LOVES me!

I kiss his neck, "I love you more, Freedom. You set me free with your love."

He pulls my hair, so I am forced to look at him.

It makes me want to ride him again.

"Marry me, Angel?! Let me keep you free."

33

Jared

Sara loves me.

Sara loves a country gangster.

I asked her to marry me; I never felt like this before.

My love for Sharon is different from my love for Sara.

This Angel hopped off my lap, grabbed the cloth that they provided, and cleaned me.

That is usually my job; I always clean her and tuck her into bed with me.

She looks at me with admiration, "When? There's no doubt in my mind I am free with you."

I caress her face, "Now. There's a chapel upstairs in the back. Kass thought it would be a nice touch."

Angel pulls on her dress, "Lead the way, sir. I will love you forever."

I stand up and zip my pants, "And I will always love you."

We head upstairs let Love's Freedom commence.

34

Terrence

I was so fucking pissed and turned on at the same time.

Sara pleasured that old man like there was no tomorrow.

Where the fuck did she learn all that?

She would never give me head.

She pleasured him like a professional.

I couldn't take my eyes off them.

As my playmate was riding me, I was picturing Sara.

Fuck I need to fuck Sara again!

She belongs with me.

I push the playmate off me and dismiss her; she knows the routine.

Where did they go?

Fuck!

I was so caught up in my thoughts I didn't see where they went.

It's okay I'll go back to the apartment complex, they will be back in the morning.

Old man, get ready your days are fucking numbered.

I can't wait to put my 22 caliber in his chest!

No one defiles what is mine!

35

Jared

"**I** now pronounce you Mr. and Mrs. Carson! You may now kill the bride!"

I grip Sara's face like my lifeline, her lips are soft and taste like supple cherries.

I never want our moment to end.

We both have lost so much.

We deserve this slice of happiness.

"You're officially mine forever, love." I say as I kiss her neck.

She smiles at me, "Does that make Freedom's Love?"

She giggles like a schoolgirl.

"No, love. You're the boss, so I'm Love's Freedom. You're corny and cute." I retort.

She snuggles into my chest, "That's perfect because you set me free from my past. Never again will I be shy, and hide who I am. I love you, Freedom."

I whisper in her ear, "I love you more. Let's go back to the hotel before we have to head home with your dad. As soon as we get back, I'll get you a ring. Also, I want to ask. Are you okay with a tracker necklace like all the Bratva women have?"

She looks at me with a wicked smile, "Are you trying to mark me, Freedom? Because I am down, that's hot! But it has to be dainty and the colors of freedom."

"As you wish, love."

I have a feeling I'll never get bored with her.

36

Terrence

Four months later...

That fucking old man and his crew.

I've been hiding for months!

Apparently, Eric Rossi recognized me when I visited him.

There's a hit out on me.

They even took out Mark!

How the fuck was I supposed to know who I was dealing with.

I may be hiding, but before I disappeared, I installed some inconspicuous cameras outside and inside Sara's house.

Because of these cameras, I know her dad's routine like the back of my hand. He goes to work every day except Saturday and Sunday.

Apparently, he works at some diner called Don's. What kind of name is that?

I have a plan to get him in a few days time.

Sara will come to rescue dear old dad and she will be mine.

All the sex Sara and her, whatever he is, has been having is both a turn-on and disgusting!

I placed a camera right outside their window, it's disguised as a bird.

They have sex almost every damn day!

You think in his old age he would be too tired for that!

But even Sara takes charge and they fuck like bunnies.

She never had a sex drive like that with me!

All these weird ass positions they like to do, what the hell!

One night I watched them fuck for one and a half hours straight!

How does he have the stamina to do that?

It's going to be hard to reign her back in.

He has made her into such a slut.

I will fix her, even if I have to rape her.

She has had her fun.

It's time for her to take her place as my slave and wife.

37

Jared

Three days later....

Life is good.

Sara and I have adjusted to married life.

We have a routine that works for us.

She is so loving and caring, and even though I tell her not to she always puts my needs before hers.

Her love is in matched.

Today is our day off; we are heading to pick up her tracking necklace.

I want her safe since her ex is still on the loose.

Love never takes her wedding set off, unless she has to perform surgery.

She opted for a rose gold vintage engagement ring, with a rose gold eternity wedding band.

She didn't want anything too flashy, the total carats is 2.5.

She only had one request for her necklace: to be the color of freedom.

So her necklace is individual hearts strung together in alternating colors.

Rubies.

Diamonds.

Sapphires.

Only the best for my wife.

As we make our way to the jewelry store, hand in hand, she just looks at me and smiles.

Love looks good on us both.

Nothing can take my love away.

38

Sara

Four hours later...

Jared got called away to go help Massimo for a while.

I can't stop staring at my ring and my necklace.

I'm not a material girl, but it's nice to feel wanted and loved.

Things with Dad have been going great, Jared and him get along great.

Dad goes to work religiously; we got him a job at Don's.

I'm walking the short distance there to go visit him at work.

As soon as I walk in the door, Matt rushes over to me.

Matt works in the kitchen, but his mainly here to keep dad safe.

"Sara, where's your dad? He didn't show up to work."

WHAT?!

I breathe deeply, "Matt, what are you talking about? He left the house before I did this morning! Why didn't you call me?"

Matt stutters, "I I figured you would be stopping by, or maybe he just needed a break. What's the big deal?"

"What's the big deal? You're part of Massimo and Jared's plan, right?" He nods, "Then don't play dumb! If anything happens to my dad, it's not Jared you have to worry about!"

I rush out the door of Don's and dial Dad's number.

Come on, pick up.

Dad, pick up!

A click, "Daddy, thank goodness! Where are you?"

"Daddy can't talk right now because you have been a bad little slut."

My blood turns ice cold.

That voice, I can't believe I am hearing it again.

"Cat got your tongue, precious? Don't worry, you don't have to speak, just listen. You're done whoring around. The old man that you're dating has got to go. If not, I kill dear old dad, and I'll put a 22 caliber round in his chest before you can say stop. Meet me at what used to be our spot, the abandoned dive bar. Be prepared to give me what I want, or Dad dies. Do you know what I want, precious? I want you—mind, body, and soul. So move your ass, or daddy will be lying next to mommy. You have twenty minutes. I love you, precious."

Click.

As soon as they hung up, I throw up.

He's back.

He wants me.

He took Dad.

He's threatening Dad.

Fuck!

I can't go back to him!

Breathe Sara!

Get your shit together.

He doesn't control you anymore.

I play with my necklace, that's it!

I dial Freedom.

He answers the first ring, "Yes, love. How can I help you?"

His voice instantly calms me.

"I love you, always. Never forget that. He's back. He took Dad. He wants me, or he will kill Dad. I know he's serious, what he's capable of, and I still have the scars to prove it. If I don't make it back, remember you deserve freedom and are capable of great love. Never let darkness reign again. Goodbye, Freedom."

Click.

I hope he forgives me.

Dad, I'm coming; I won't let him take you from me.

39

Jared

"Love, no! Wait!"

Damn it!

"Massimo! He's surfaced! Sara is going after him! Pull up the tracker! I will murder him if he touches my wife!"

I'm furious.

That SOB deserves to be six feet under!

"Calm down, brother. I'm on it. She headed to the old dive bar. Let's go get her and her dad. Nobody harms what is ours and lives to tell the tale." He pats me on the shoulder.

We rush out,

Massimo spared his life once.

I will not be as forgiving.

I'm on my way, my love.

40

Terrence

Sara does our secret knock.

Knock, knock.

Knock, knock, knock.

"Enter, precious."

Sara enters, "Let my dad go. I'll do what you want."

I would do anything for her.

"Kiss me, and I'll set him free."

I see the regret in her eyes as she steps forward.

She puts her hands on my shoulders and pecks me on the cheek.

So that's how she wants to play it.

"Mr. Rossi, you're free to go. I hope to see you again soon."

I cut his wrists free; he whispers something to Sara.

She replies, "I love you, Daddy."

Eric leaves.

"Get on your knees, Sara. You have years to make up for. You decided you didn't need me. So you deserve everything that I am about to do to you."

I have struck a nerve; the fear reaches her eyes.

"Terrence, you have tortured me enough for eternity. You killed our baby! You never tried to apologize, and I almost died too. But you didn't care about that. All you cared about was your image."

How dare she!

Smack!

"How dare you! If you had been the obedient little fiancée, there would have been no problems! But you had to fuck everything up and get pregnant! I never wanted kids! I still despise them! If you would have got rid of the little demon when I told you to, I wouldn't had to cut it out of you!"

Tears sting her eyes, "You killed my little girl! You killed a little angel! I can never love you again! You're the epitome of a monster!"

Smack!

Smack!

She can't take my smacks across her jaw anymore.

This time, she falls to her knees.

"That's where you belong, whore."

I unzip my pants and stroke my cock.

"Precious, I will give you one last chance to obey before I fuck you into submission."

She looks up at me, tears flowing down her face.

She doesn't speak, she spits on my cock.

I grab her by her hair, "Fight me all you want; I'm taking what's mine!"

I rip her blouse open and tear her skirt in pieces.

"Please Terrence!" she cries. "If you ever loved me, don't do this! Just let me go! You can move far away, and we will forget our entire past!"

I cackle, "Never, precious! You're only mine! I will take what belongs to me one last time, and we will die together!"

I rip her panties from her legs and straddle her; just as I'm about to enter her the door swings open.

"Get off my wife!"

It's the old man!

WIFE!

I look at her ring finger; there sits a wedding set.

What a slut!

She was going to let me fuck her.

"Your wife came onto me, old man. Take it up with her."

I slowly get off Sara.

My gun is in my back pocket.

It's a good thing I didn't remove my jeans.

It's time for the old man to die.

41

Jared

This deranged man is going to die tonight right now.

Out of the corner of my eye, I see Sara crawling out the door.

Go, my love.

Massimo is right outside.

Massimo knows my plan.

Arson leaves no evidence.

Massimo is getting Eric and Sara to safety.

I've already doused the perimeter of the building with gasoline.

The haunting of Sara ends now.

Terrence points his 22 at me, "Are you ready to die for your slut of a wife?"

I take two steps forward toward him, "Are you ready to die because you touched another man's wife? I do not share, and I'm sure Sara told you no."

He laughs, "You would kill me for a piece of pussy?"

I take two more steps forward, "No, I would kill you for free." Two more steps forward, he hasn't noticed yet. "You have traumatized an angel! She never deserved what you put her through, but I'm here to set her free from her past."

He cocks his pistol, "And how are you going to do that, old man?"

I grin.

I pull out my gun from my waistband.

I smash his nose with the butt of my pistol, "Same way you were trying to get her back. Murder, you touch what's mine, you die!"

One shot was all I needed, and the bullet went straight through his heart.

I wiped the gun clean and placed it in his dead hand.

I head outside.

I light my cigar and throw it to the ground.

I don't have to look back.

I feel the flames reaching the sky.

My Love is free.

42

Epilogue-Sara

*T*wo months later....

I no longer work at the hospital.

After the trauma at the hands of Terrence, again, I decided it was time for me to take a break.

Jared and I have been going to therapy together.

We are working on us.

We are bettering ourselves for each other.

Jared has been more forthcoming with his thoughts and emotions.

He hasn't disassociated in almost two months.

I know he killed Terrence.

Does that bother me?

No, Jared's goodness outweighs his sins.

He and the entire Bratva family do more good than crime.

I could get used to being part of this family.

Jared spoils me, apparently, that's a trend with all Bratva men.

I am free.

My new freedom is precious; I will not take it for granted.

It's all because of Jared.

I'm his Love, he's my Freedom.

Love's Freedom is red, white, and blue.

Free but with sacrifice.

THE END

Author's Note

Thank you for reading!
   I hope you enjoyed my fictional world!
   Stay safe, and remember, life is what you make it, so make it fiction!

From one reader to another, support your independent authors and bookstores!

Lots of love,
Summer N Dawn

About the Author

A small-town independent author just trying to live out her dream.

She wants to bring joy to everyone she can.

She has cerebral palsy but never lets that stop her.

Life is meant to be enjoyed, so she writes her books so others can escape into a world everyone can fit into.